# Letters From a Self-made Merchant to his Son

# Letters from
# A Self-Made Merchant
# To His Son

Being some of the letters written by John Graham, head of
the House of Graham & Company, Pork Packers in
Chicago, familiarly known on 'Change as "Old Gorgon
Graham," to his son, Pierrepont, facetiously known to his
intimates as "Piggy."

*By*

*GEORGE HORACE LORIMER*

—

## Written in Gregg Shorthand
*Revised Edition*

—

Published by permission of
SMALL, MAYNARD & COMPANY, BOSTON

## The Gregg Publishing Company
New York    Chicago    Boston    San Francisco
London

Shorthand Plates Written by
GEORGIE GREGG

H-55-PP-3
Ch

# Preface

ONE of the most interesting and helpful books published in recent years is "LETTERS from a SELF-MADE MERCHANT to his son," *by George Horace Lorimer.* We read these letters with much pleasure when they were appearing in serial form and made use of them—as did many other teachers—in giving advanced dictation to shorthand students. They were a welcome relief from the monotony of continuous dictation of business papers and correspondence, and at the same time they enforced many valuable lessons in such a way as to impress them vividly upon the minds of the students. The dictation of something in a lighter vein is desirable occasionally, and for this purpose there could be nothing more suitable than the letters contained in this book.

Recently William Marion Reedy, in an article about the *Saturday Evening Post,* which has been edited by Mr. Lorimer for many years said:

> George Horace Lorimer is the world's greatest editor. Lorimer's "Letters from a Self-made Merchant to his Son" is the best piece of pragmatic philosophy since Ben Franklin, who founded the *Saturday Evening Post.*

In issuing this selection of letters from the original book, we we desire to acknowledge our indebtedness to the publishers, Messrs. Small, Maynard and Company, for permission to use a certain number of these letters in this way, and also to the artists, B. Martin Justice and F. R. Gruger, for the use of some of the illustrations.

To those who enjoy reading these letters we heartily commend the complete work, which contains a number of others equally entertaining and helpful.

THE GREGG PUBLISHING COMPANY

# CONTENTS

# CONTENTS—*Continued*

## No. 1

FROM John Graham, at the Union Stock Yards in Chicago, to his son, Pierrepont, at Harvard University, Cambridge, Mass. Mr. Pierrepont has just been settled by his mother as a member, in good and regular standing, of the Freshman class.

*"Old Doc Hoover asked me right out in Sunday School if I didn't want to be saved."*

*(shorthand text — not transcribable)*

# No. 2

FROM John Graham, at the Union Stock Yards in Chicago, to his son, Pierrepont, at Harvard University. Mr. Pierrepont's expense account has just passed under his father's eye, and has furnished him with a text for some plain particularities.

*"I have seen hundreds of boys go to Europe who didn't bring back a great deal except a few trunks of badly fitting clothes."*

60'

106'

## No. 3

FROM John Graham, at the Union Stock Yards in Chicago, to his son, Pierrepont, at Harvard University. Mr. Pierrepont finds Cambridge to his liking, and has suggested that he take a post-graduate course to fill up some gaps which he has found in his education.

"*I put Jim Durham out on the
road to introduce a new product.*"

# III

## No. 4

FROM John Graham, head of the house of Graham & Co., at the Union Stock Yards in Chicago, to his son, Pierrepont Graham, at the Waldorf-Astoria, in New York. Mr. Pierrepont has suggested the grand tour as a proper finish to his education.

"Old Dick Stover was the worst hand
at procrastinating that I ever saw."

# IV

*25, 189—*

## No. 5

FROM John Graham, head of the house of Graham & Co., at the Union Stock Yards in Chicago, to his son, Pierrepont Graham, at Lake Moosgatchemawamuc, in the Maine woods. Mr. Pierrepont has written to his father withdrawing his suggestion.

*"Charlie Chase told me he was President of the Klondike Exploring, Gold Prospecting and Immigration Company."*

# V

## No. 10

**F**ROM John Graham, at the Union Stock Yards in Chicago, to his son, Pierrepont, at the Commercial House, Jeffersonville, Indiana. Mr. Pierrepont has been promoted to the position of traveling salesman for the house, and has started out on the road.

*"You looked so blamed important and chesty when you started off."*

# X

## No. 11

FROM John Graham, at the Union Stock Yards in Chicago, to his son, Pierrepont, at The Planters' Palace Hotel, at Big Gap, Kentucky. Mr. Pierrepont's orders are small and his expenses are large, so his father feels pessimistic over his prospects.

*"Josh Jenkinson would eat a little food now and then just to be sociable, but what he really lived on was tobacco."*

## No. 13

FROM John Graham, at the Union Stock Yards in Chicago, to his son, Pierrepont, care of The Hoosier Grocery Co., Indianapolis, Indiana. Mr. Pierrepont's orders have been looking up, so the old man gives him a pat on the back—but not too hard a one.

*"When John L. Sullivan went through the stock yards, it just simply shut down the plant."*

# XIII

*[shorthand text]*

93

## No. 15

FROM John Graham, at the Union Stock Yards in Chicago, to his son, Pierrepont, at The Scrub Oaks, Spring Lake, Michigan. Mr. Pierrepont has been promoted again, and the old man sends him a little advice with his appointment.

*"A good many salesmen have an idea
that buyers are only interested in funny
stories."*

# XV

# SOME GREGG PUBLICATIONS

*(Prices subject to change without notice)*

### SHORTHAND INSTRUCTION BOOKS

**Gregg Shorthand Manual.** Revised edition. Bound in cloth...$1.50

**Gregg Speed Studies.** Combined supplementary textbook and dictation course, dealing with problems of speed and accuracy. All reading and writing material in shorthand, conforming to principles of the New Manual. 328 pages, cloth binding ....... 1.20

**Supplementary Exercises in Gregg Shorthand.** A collection of words, sentences, letters, tests and charts in shorthand and type, arranged in accordance with the division of material in the Revised Manual. 62 pages................................. .60

**Progressive Exercises in Gregg Shorthand.** Revised for use with the New Manual. Tests students' knowledge of each lesson .. .50

**Graded Readings in Gregg Shorthand.** By Alice M. Hunter. A new reading book adapted to early dictation. 120 pages, cloth binding..................................................... .75

**Lessons in Shorthand Penmanship.** By John Robert Gregg ... .12

**Gregg Speed Practice.** Reading and writing exercises, combined with dictation practice. Illustrated with shorthand forms. 258 pages.................................................... 1.20

**Gregg Shorthand Dictionary.** New edition, containing the outlines of nearly 17,000 words. Flexible binding................. 1.50

**Gregg Shorthand Phrase Book.** Contains about 2,400 useful phrases. A great aid in attaining speed. Vest-pocket size .. .75

**Practical Drills in Shorthand Penmanship.** By George S. McClure................................................... .16

**Curso de Taquigrafia de Gregg.** (An adaptation of Gregg Shorthand to Spanish.) Bound in cloth...................... 1.50

**Gregg Shorthand Adapted to Esperanto.** By Ernest L. Jackson. Attractively bound ................................... .40

### DICTATION

**Expert Shorthand Speed Course.** By Rupert P. SoRelle. Explains the methods and gives the practice matter used in training the successful contestants for the Miner Medal. 260 pages, bound in cloth.................................................... 1.00

**Graded Dictation.** By Walter Rasmussen. Carefully graded, with blanks for writing in the shorthand. 228 pages........... 1.00

**Shorthand Dictation Drills.** Edited by John Robert Gregg. Carefully graded dictation material — business letters, literary and informative articles. Printed entirely in type. Bound in cloth. 212 pages...................................... .80

**Constructive Dictation.** By Edward Hall Gardner. Embodies a new idea of teaching practical business English along with dictation. Extensive vocabulary in shorthand. 376 pages. Cloth .... 1.20

# FOR THE REPORTER

**The Gregg Reporter.** By John Robert Gregg. A guide to court reporting, with list of reporting phrases and short cuts, plates of court testimony, etc. 111 pages, bound in cloth.................$1.50

**Gregg Court Reporting Series.** Practice matter on court testimony, jury charges, etc. **Gregg Notes Nos. 1 and 2** are the shorthand forms: **Gregg Dictation Nos. 1 and 2** are the transscripts. Each pamphlet.................................... .24

**Gregg Reporting Shortcuts.** By John Robert Gregg............ 2.25

## READING BOOKS IN GREGG SHORTHAND

**Gregg Shorthand Reader.** A collection of stories and articles .... .28

**The Sign of the Four.** By Sir A. Conan Doyle., 188 pages bound in cloth..................................... .75

**Letters from a Self-Made Merchant to His Son.** By George Horace Lorimer. Revised edition, 120 pages, bound in cloth..... .75

**Creeds of Great Business Men.** 38 pages..................... .24

**A Christmas Carol.** By Charles Dickens. 56 pages............ .28

**The Great Stone Face.** By Nathaniel Hawthorne.............. .24

**The Legend of Sleepy Hollow.** By Washington Irving.......... .32

**Rip Van Winkle.** By Washington Irving...................... .28

**Hamlet.** As told by Charles Lamb........................... .20

**Alice in Wonderland.** By Lewis Carroll. 154 pages............ .75

**Advanced Practice in Gregg Shorthand.** Three Parts. The shorthand version of the articles in "Expert Shorthand Speed Course." Each part......................................... .50

## TYPEWRITING

**Rational Typewriting.** By Rupert P. SoRelle and Ida McLenan Cutler. Cloth bound, end opening.

**Revised Edition.** A comprehensive course for use in high schools and private business schools desiring an extended course ........ 1.50

**Medal of Honor Edition.** A short, intensive course for highly specialized business schools.................................. 1.08

**Methods of Teaching Typewriting.** By Rupert P. SoRelle. Net 1.50

**Typewriting Speed Studies.** By Adelaide B. Hakes .......... .52

## ENGLISH, SPELLING

**Applied Business English and Correspondence.** By Hubert A. Hagar and Rupert P. SoRelle. Teacher's key furnished.
Commercial School Edition (exercises included). 344 pages... 1.40
High School Edition (without exercises). 190 pages.......... 1.00
Separate Exercises for use with High School Edition.......... .40

**Applied Business Correspondence and Punctuation.** 110 pages. .75
Separate Exercises in Punctuation ...................... .20

**Words: Their Spelling, Pronunciation, Definition and Application.** A new idea in spelling texts. 162 pages, bound in cloth .44

## OFFICE TRAINING

**Office Training for Stenographers.** By Rupert P. SoRelle. A complete and practical secretarial course for the advanced shorthand department, with separate Exercise Book. Text, $1.25; Exercises, 75c.................................................. 2.00

## COMMERCIAL SUBJECTS

**Essentials of Commercial Law.** By Wallace H. Whigam. Cloth bound, 392 pages..................................$1.40

**Walsh's Business Arithmetic.** By John H. Walsh, Associate Superintendent of Schools, New York. For high schools and commercial schools. 496 pages. Cloth.................. 1.40

**Rational Arithmetic.** By George P. Lord ........................ 1.00

**Lockyear's Bookkeeping.** By M. H. Lockyear. An introductory course. Cloth bound, 105 pages................................. .80

**Bartholomew's Bookkeeping Exercises.** By W. E. Bartholomew. Constructive problems adapted to any text. In two parts, each.. .72

**Applied Business Calculation.** By C. E. Birch. 193 pages... .40

## MISCELLANEOUS

**Business Organization and Administration.** By J. Anton de Hass 1.40

**An Introduction to Economics.** By Graham A. Laing. 400 pages........................................................ 1.40

**The Teaching of Shorthand: Some Suggestions to Young Teachers.** By John Robert Gregg............................. .75

**Vocabulary of the Manual.** A complete alphabetical list of all the words contained in the revised edition of the Gregg Shorthand Manual. 54 pages................................................ .60

**How to Prepare for Civil Service.** By E. H. Cooper. Cloth.... 1.50

**The Factors of Shorthand Speed.** By David Wolfe Brown. 194 pages, cloth bound...................................... .75

**Practical Pointers for Shorthand Students.** By Frank Rutherford. 131 pages, cloth bound.................................. .50

**The Parliamentarian.** By Cora Welles Trow. A manual of parliamentary procedure and the rules of debate. 158 pages, cloth bound.............................................. .75

**Personality: Studies in Personal Development.** By Harry Collins Spillman. A book that opens a new field in education. Adapted to corporation schools, high schools and self-study. 206 pages, cloth bound.................................... 1.50

**The Gregg Emblem.** The Gregg ovals in blue and white enamel, with gold lettering. Pin or button.......................... .50

**The Gregg Notebook.** Specially prepared for Gregg writers. Size 6x8¾ inches. Price in quantities quoted on application.

**Gregg Reporter's Notebook**...................................... .20

**Expert Copy Holder.** For typewriting manuals................... 1.00

**Wall Charts.** The Gregg Alphabet in blue print, mounted map style. Four charts, 30x39 inches ...........................Net 2.50

**The Gregg Pennant.** Of blue and white felt, 18x36 inches........ 1.50

**The Gregg Eraser Tray.** Bronze finish........................ .50

# *The Gregg Publishing Company*

NEW YORK    CHICAGO    BOSTON    SAN FRANCISCO    LONDON

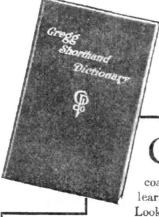

# Add These 16,000 Words to Your Shorthand Vocabulary

CARRY this handy little book in your coat pocket or your handbag and learn a few new outlines each day. Look up the form for the unusual word you come across in your reading. Be sure that you write the shortest outline for the new words you encounter in dictation. Be ready for a position in a different line of work if it is offered you.

Nothing is of greater importance in increasing speed than a large shorthand vocabulary, and there is no surer or easier way of acquiring one than by the consistent use of the

# Gregg Shorthand Dictionary

The Dictionary contains nearly three times as many words as the former edition. They have been carefully chosen with a view to their frequency of use and the shorthand outlines are beautifully written in conformity with the principles of the new Manual.

It is just the right size to slip into the coat pocket and is beautifully bound in brown cloth, side-stamped in gold.

208 pages.........................$1.50

## The Gregg Publishing Company

NEW YORK   CHICAGO   BOSTON   SAN FRANCISCO   LONDON